Dreadful Delicacies

Photographs by Al Clayton
Text and Styling by Mary Ann Clayton

LONGSTREET PRESS
Atlanta, Georgia

Published by
LONGSTREET PRESS, INC.
A subsidiary of Cox Newspapers,
A division of Cox Enterprises, Inc.
2140 Newmarket Parkway
Suite 118
Marietta, GA 30067

Printed in the United States of America

1st printing 1993

Library of Congress Catalog Card Number: 93-79664

ISBN 1-56352-093-1

This book was printed by Semline, Incorporated, Braintree, Massachusetts.

Jacket design by Jill Dible
Book design and typesetting by Laura McDonald

To the Flint Hill Egg Hunters
With love and affection

Carnivore: Eats meat

Herbivore: Eats plants

Insectivore: Eats insects

Omnivore: Eats anything

Contents

More than half the world's labor force is involved in food production. Providing food has always been the major occupation of humankind.

Preface

Very few people are neutral on the subject of cultural food prejudices. Some would push every known boundary of "socially correct" dining; others would restrict intake to the most bland and simple fare necessary to maintain life. Most of us land somewhere in between these extremes. Hopefully each of us can be accepting of others' choices. ❧ Perhaps many of today's prejudices come from being so far removed from the source of our food. Most children think milk comes from plastic gallon containers in the grocery store. What would they think if they knew it came from a cow's udder? Would they still drink it or would it become something revolting? ❧ How would they react to the news that the delectable golden honey on their breakfast toast is actually a combination of flower nectar and bee spit? Would the little darlings gurgle red cubes of squiggly cherry-flavored gelatin down their throats if they knew that one of its ingredients came from the foot of a cow? ❧ And those little jars of pale pasty goop that toddlers wolf down—do they care whether they are eating chicken innards or broccoli? Probably not. ❧ If left to make their own choices, small children will usually eat anything. You've seen them, I know, in the sandbox scooping up and munching with gustatory delight the leavings of the family pet. We have to tell them that pet droppings are not delicious and that they will be socially ostracized if they do not change their dietary habits before reaching adulthood. Although there may be an innate dislike for the taste or texture of some foods, I doubt it. I think we eat what is acceptable in our group to eat—first what we are served in our family, later the favorites of our friends and still later, we may accept the foods of other cultures.   Unfortunately, many of us never get beyond the first one or two groups and therefore cheat ourselves of the gastronomic pleasures available to us. Why else would we search for a fish that doesn't taste fishy, or sigh in relief when we can proclaim that the alligator tail tastes just like chicken? Is it because a chicken or a flounder is more socially acceptable than the alligator or river catfish?   Trying to answer such questions can provide us with some very humorous and thoughtful insights about ourselves and our world and unite us in the never-ending quest to know:

Why do we eat what we eat?

Thanks

Anytime one accomplishes something, like having a book published, there are a zillion people to be thanked for their support and encouragement, and we do thank them all. A few of these zillion were most closely associated with us during the process of creating this book: Our families, Chuck Mumah, Mac Talmadge, Terry Colby, John Egerton, Marianne deHaan and the Ladies Who Breakfast. We would like to give particular thanks to Kay and Buck Goldstein, Susan Mack, Jonathan Shils, Andy Armstrong, and Judith Stogner for their generous support. We are most grateful to our wonderful children for their insightful suggestions and for sticking with us all these years. Special thanks to our editor and indexer extraordinaire, Suzanne Bell; to Chuck Perry, Jill Dible, Laura McDonald, and the whole wonderful staff at Longstreet Press, especially Beverly Morgan and Ruth Waters, who suffered graciously under the expressed anxieties of my husband (I, of course, keep a calm demeanor). And thanks to our main sources of material, the Sweet Auburn Curb Market and various and sundry bait shops and farmers markets around the state of Georgia.

*J*ohn had his raiment of camel's
hair, and a leathern girdle about his loins; and
his meat was locusts and wild honey.

— *Matthew 3:4*

Introduction

Chasing birds, insects and small animals away from my garden and orchard was sapping too much of my energy, so about a year ago I got the bright idea of including these critters in my harvest—lettuce, tomatoes, beetles, cucumbers—and putting them all to use. Right there I created a beautiful salad of organically grown produce with the added crunchy nutrition of a few beetles. It was win-win. The beetles were delicious, and with fewer of them left to wreak havoc in the garden, my produce yield was the most and best I ever had. Inspired by my own ingenuity, I began compiling a collection of very unusual recipes using very ordinary ingredients—all one needed to do was walk out the back door (or the front) and gather what was wanted. I was sure I had the only original idea to come down the pike in years. Imagine my surprise when I began reading (I am an avid reader) in magazines and newspapers about a sizable number of other people who are interested in the same things. ❦ At first I was quite miffed that my pursuit was not unique, but then I became excited that this idea is universal. It's as though we have all absorbed some important cosmic information that we are each trying to transform into a workable means of feeding the earth's population. Each of us has her or his own special talents and viewpoint and each of us will hopefully make a positive difference. ❧ We are constantly looking for new grains, produce and meats to include in our culinary repertoire. We are relearning the concept of utilizing every part of the animals we use for food, even those "awful offals," so labeled by my maiden aunts, Abigail and Mary Margaret (they're on my daddy's side of the family). We need look no further than our own backyards. This method of assembling a meal from what is available in one's immediate environment is as ancient as woman and man themselves. Isn't this what our ancestors did? They gathered berries and insects and hunted animals. They had no supermarket to provide plastic-wrapped skinless boneless chicken breasts. How do we know what is *really* in there when we can see no chicken characteristic to help us identify the pale rectangles of flesh lying on the white Styrofoam trays? We have to take the store's label on faith; there are not even any real butchers to assist us. ❧ I have been observing closely the patterns of food trends of this past year, searching for a way to spread my message of nutritional and environmental concerns. Basically, I have learned that anything that originates in California will at some point sweep through the whole United States like a storm of locusts. I don't live in California but I think I can help turn the tide—and this time, with your participation, it will be a nationwide explosion. At this very moment, in the Midwest, scientists are developing methods of farming insects for human consumption.

Believe me. I am telling you the truth. And each and every one of you can support this movement by becoming aware of the bounty that lies at your very fingertips (or toetips). ✴ Without prejudice and preconceived notions, but with an open mind and a willingness to explore, we can improve our health and our environment simultaneously. Have no fear. All that is offered here may not be familiar to you, but be assured it is a delicacy, if not a staple, on someone's dinner table somewhere. ✴ My Yankee neighbors scorn grits and I feel sorry for them. It's just that, as children, they were deprived of the pleasure of steaming mounds of these grains adorned with puddles of melting butter and sprinkles of ground black pepper. Mmmmmmm! Because they are not familiar with grits, have no sentimental or gustatory memories of grits, they do not want to eat grits. As my sister-in-law, Kathy, says, "It all boils down to what you're used to." I say, "Amen, thank God," I am used to grits. ✴ However, I'm not used to some of the foods that have come to my attention over the past couple of years, but, as my husband says, one of my most endearing attributes is an open mind. I am willing to experiment and remain receptive to the possibilities. Within the pages of this book are not recipes but guides that are meant to encourage your own creative ideas. All I ask is that you join me as a fellow explorer on this culinary journey. Enjoy!

Dreadful Delicacies

En Gel

As you have probably noticed, I am trying to learn some languages other than American English. (I even thought of taking a course of English as a second language when I was in London—it sounds so different over there.) Soon the whole world will be speaking English as well as their own native tongues, which puts us at a disadvantage—they understand us but we don't necessarily understand them. I have done my own titles for several of my creations that are included in this book. I think they are very clever and quite amusing. Little Jenny Lynn's pronunciation of this beautiful dessert translates to "Angels," and that is what we call it at our house.

My mother, Nancy Eugenia Malcomb, used to make huge bowls of sweet fruity gelatin cubes covered with great globs of soft whipped cream on top. Paul David, my oldest brother, would suck the cold quivering chunks through his front teeth, the whipped cream leaving a sugary white mustache on his upper lip. It helped that he always seemed to be lacking one of those teeth. I think the surprises in my version of Mother's memorable treat might have slowed him down though.

Everyone likes to experiment with the lovely garnishes and the flavors and colors in the gelatin. Some like the purity of one solid shimmering color—others want to see how many palettes they can create. But all succeed in creating beautiful food art. The worms and the gelatin also make En Gel a very high protein item. If the worms give you a problem, just think of how the gelatin is made.

Eyes of Texas Enchilada

Never ask anyone to tell you the strangest thing he's ever eaten . . . you don't really want to know. Before I learned this lesson, I used to ask people that question all the time. I thought I *did* want to know. Well, the food most often mentioned was eyes—eyes of monkeys, birds, cows, pigs, you name it—usually encountered when the partaker was in a culture where it is considered an honor to be offered the eyes of the main course and an affront to refuse them.

My husband's friend Chucker is always singing songs about Texas. I don't know why, I'm not even sure he's ever been to Texas. Still, his yowling did suggest the name of this dish and got my creative juices flowing. Just imagine yourself as a guest on a multi-thousand-acre ranch when breakfast arrives and the host says, "We butchered us a steer yesterday and because we are so pleased to have you with us we saved the eyes for you." Buena cucina!

Feetballs

This "picnic" basket has held schoolwork, stationery and baby diapers and now has been claimed by the sports spectators. The red and black blanket goes back to my husband's college days. I'm sure he has memories of it that I don't want to know. The pom-poms are from my high school cheerleading adventures. I keep them stored with mothballs in Davison's Department Store boxes along with my majorette boots. (I was a very energetic girl in high school.)

Now we are into some deep stuff! Personally, I don't know why this dish evokes such horror and fascination in the men to whom it is presented, but my psychoanalyst friend, Mick, says that the basis of the human male's psyche is the fear of someone hurting his maleness, if you know what I mean.

Well, just serve this menu at a football tailgate party, and every man in the parking lot will come over to see and perhaps sample it; not one of them will fail to comment on the size of the rooster's prizes. They are merely getting in touch with their primal selves . . . experiencing the ultimate terror and, in the milieu of a macho game of body bruising, somehow coming to terms with their inner masculinity. It's either that or going out into the woods and beating on some drums.

Fettuccine Mater Terra

I have been served "fettuccine" that was actually julienne of pigs' ears. I swear it! Little strips of cartilage in a light lemon sauce. I cannot tell you how much my world has broadened in the last few years. I have been to London and to Paris and to Rome, all within ten glorious days. Oh, the things I saw and heard and the food I saw and/or tasted (I never said I didn't have my own food prejudices, but I am working hard to dispel them). And I want to share my enlightenment with you by creating culinary combinations that will inspire you just as I have been inspired by my expanded consciousness.

In Venice, at a tiny, family-owned restaurant on a side canal street, my husband was presented with the house special, Rissoto Mater Domini (he still calls it Mother of God Casserole). The rissoto, a short-grained Italian rice, had a blackish sauce made from squid and its "ink" sac. It was quite salty and tasted exactly as one might expect of the *frutti de mer*. (As you can see, I am on a linguistic adventure, also.)

Just as Risotto Mater Domini is the fruit of the sea, Fettuccine Mater Terra is truly the bounty of Mother Earth: semolina pasta, exotic oyster mushrooms and earthworms.

Only a little chopped parsley is added so as not to mask the musty flavors of the moist undergrowth of the forest. This dish could be served with no apologies in the finest restaurant. On the other hand, it is a wonderful meal for outdoor campers, who need to take only the dried pasta with them since everything else can be gathered while they are hiking around. Versatility is my forte!

$\mathcal{I}$nsects are the largest group of animals
on earth, outnumbering humans by thousands
and outweighing us more than 10 to 1.
(Have you hugged your bug today?)

Four and Twenty Blackbirds

Sing a song of sixpence
A pocket full of rye
Four and twenty blackbirds
Baked in a pie.

When the pie was opened
The birds began to sing
Wasn't that a dainty dish
To set before a king?

Even if you didn't know that I have been to England, this dish would be a dead
giveaway. It is inspired, of course, by that old nursery rhyme about the king and the
queen and all their money and their servants, and their eating habits. Four and Twenty
Blackbirds is my interpretation of how that legendary blackbird pie may have looked
two or three hundred years ago.

As paranoid as kings seemed to be back then, I am sure this one would have
demanded to see exactly what he was eating and not have it covered up with a heavy,
doughy crust. My delicate puff pastry holds the bird gently in a rich Marsala sauce

studded with colorful vegetables and flavored with rosemary, which grows in profusion beside my back doorsteps. It is served in Miss Claire's English pottery bowl on a cloth embroidered by my cousin, "Fafa" Anita. The fruit-patterned drapery in the background was handprinted by my talented friend Sara Andy, who loves beautiful things about as much as I do. I made the satin coin purse to look like one I saw in a London museum, an excellent copy if I do say so myself.

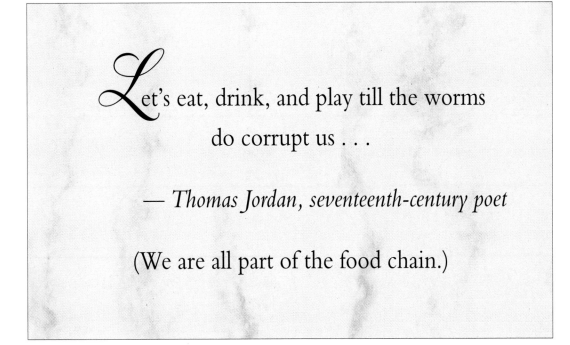

*L*et's eat, drink, and play till the worms

do corrupt us . . .

— *Thomas Jordan, seventeenth-century poet*

(We are all part of the food chain.)

Grubons

Is there a lunch more inviting on a hot summer day than a dewy salad picked right from your own garden? The only thing that could make it better is the addition of some grubs that have been sautéed in extra-virgin olive oil and sprinkled over the greens to add a salty crunch. So while you are out there harvesting the lettuces, don't discard the little pests that are feeding on your vegetables.

I like to take my brimming garden basket (I wove it myself with vines from the wisteria that twines over the garden shed) directly to my kitchen sink and wash greens and grubs with lots of cool water. A loosely woven white cotton tea towel over a cool marble counter top is a perfect place to dry them. If the grubs have been feeding on your chemical-free lettuces, you can use them right away. You know firsthand that they have had a cleaner, purer diet than a lobster or a crab or even a free-range chicken.

My husband is an intuitive sort of person — you might even say impetuous. He does love to eat and has become quite interested in my exploration of new (to us) worlds of gastronomy. That man can come up with some doozie ideas. I, of course, have a more analytical nature, and it is up to me to consider the feasibility of his impulsiveness. He thinks I am so clever when I come up with one of my "ecologically correct" solutions to universal problems. He is now looking for investors in my new culinary discovery — I am agreeable to that endeavor. Now he wants to package and market these garnishes and has given them a cute name in a catchy phrase, "Forget the croutons, pour on the Grubons!"

Hams and Eggs

Most recipes for whole crickets suggest removing the legs before eating. This seems like a terrible waste to me (you know how frugal I am), so I have tried to think of some recipes that utilize these leftover parts.

Because our son Kevin (who will someday be Dr. Kevin) would never eat eggs, I thought this might be an opportunity to entice him with a breakfast of soft scrambled eggs and crisp, meaty little hams from the crickets. One must be careful swallowing them, however—I have heard that they can get stuck in your throat. The succulent eggs should assist them on their alimentary journey.

Liver and Lace

My friend Weeze is always thinking up adventurous romantic trysts with her very appreciative husband. The other day, though, she drew a blank trying to plan an anniversary dinner. Luckily she came to me for advice. Even quiet romantic dinners for two can be boring because many times we serve the same old thing, something expected, some favorite dish of the person we are courting. Why not zonk him with something really special, something he has never associated with romance.

This tripe, poached in minted broth, makes a lacy background for the yummy candied sweet potatoes and thin, thin, thin calf's liver shaped into hearts with a cookie cutter. Chances are he will never even know it is liver; the tripe . . . maybe. The Irish thistle-and-shamrock lace cloth was part of my Grandmother Lula Wiley's dowry, the plates were acquired at an estate auction and the wooden hearts were carved by one of my favorite men, Weeze's husband, Little Sam, to whom this dish is dedicated.

Nippon Crickets

While I myself am not a fan of raw meats of any kind, my friend Terry can make some fantastic sushi (at least it looks fantastic). She has an extensive store of serving trays and handmade chopsticks which she loaned me for this special occasion, my sister Marianne's birthday.

Terry's husband, Bob Too (his mother wouldn't let anyone call him Junior), told us about eating something similar to this when he was working in Tokyo. At first he thought the crickets were alive, then he thought they were only decorative. But when he saw the other guests ingesting them, he knew what he had to do and he did it. To his surprise he found them quite palatable. "Somewhat like potato chips," he said.

When you think about it, the soft texture of most sushi practically cries out for a crisp crunchy accent like this.

Pas de Pears

What really strikes one about this magnificent dessert is the grace and movement of the mealworms and the fluid swirl of the jewel-colored raspberry sauce, hence the name we have given it, Dance of the Pears. And it is all natural!

Because the orchard owners have already upset the balance of nature by planting great numbers of pear trees where none grew before, they must contend with the critters the fruit trees attract. But if we do our part by becoming more ecologically aware consumers, the growers will not have to use pesticides. We will not be looking at the green grocers for those perfect blemish-free fruits that cheat us of the delightful dividend of worms and insects; they only add to the elegance and nutritional value of our desserts. Can't you just hear your family chanting, "We want evidence of residents!"

P.B. & J.

Some of my most successful concoctions are based on old favorites like this peanut butter and jelly sandwich to which I have added french-fried crickets. Decoratively sliced apples complete a well-balanced meal.

On Saturdays our son Galen, who has the voice of an angel, loves to take this to his choir practice. None of his fellow warblers will have a lunch half as exciting—it's guaranteed to be the hit of the noon break. The connection between the singers and the musically gifted insects is not lost on this group.

Galen likes to pack his lunch in this charming painted metal lunch box. When we have P.B. & J.'s at home, I like to decorate the table with these antique toy circus animals given to our children by Miz Nan, a dear family friend.

Pea Brain

Pea Brain, Pea Brain,
Doesn't have sense
To come in from the rain.

You've probably heard your children sing-song this unflattering ditty a hundred times—I know I have. Our youngest child, David, who was often the recipient of this verbal barrage, has turned out to be a very fine artist (he takes after me, of course). In retaliation for those taunts from his siblings, he agreed to paint this canvas tablecloth for me so that I could create a masterpiece interpretation of the heights "Pea Brain" could attain.

The poached veal brains are blanketed with a tropical mango glaze, and the peas are steamed over basil-flavored water. Mango and apple purée in pale yellow endive leaves are garnished with stems of globe basil and petals of salmon-colored geraniums. The soft luster of this aluminum cake plate adds perfect texture to our museum-quality setting. My mother, Nancy Eugenia Malcomb, has had this plate for as long as I can remember.

Pease Porridge Hot

Pease porridge hot
Pease porridge cold
Pease porridge in the pot
Nine days old.

Some like it hot
Some like it cold
Some like it in the pot
Nine days old.

O - U - T spells OUT!

Grubons again! This time as a nourishing garnish for Miss Alice's split pea soup. (My name for it comes from her favorite rhyming game. I think she took all the clapping of hands that goes with the recitation as personal applause.) Miss Alice always serves it in these bowls because she thinks the green pattern of the china makes a beautiful border for the green soup that is so thick you can almost eat it with a fork. The grubs are not included in her original recipe, but the little carrot flowers are. As soon as she can speak again I will let you know how she feels about my contribution.

You can see how versatile these little grubs are. Fortunately for those of us who find them indispensable to our larder, they are also abundantly available. There are some misguided gardeners who will even pay to have them removed from their plants . . . a wonderful summer job for the children.

$\mathcal{I}$n England you can get a side
order of mushy peas with your fish and chips.
This is an evolution of the dense soup in the
rhyme "Pease Porridge Hot."

Ratatouille

This goes to show you what my husband knows about cooking. How he can call this a vegetable stew is beyond me—maybe the zucchini and onions and tomatoes are stuffed inside the eggplant.

He and his friend Little Sam put this dish together one day when I went into town. At least that's their story. Obviously he was in my garden (very unusual), because nowhere else could he have gotten the sumptuous eggplant and the tiny bitter melon (in ratatouille?). This picture is the only clue to what they were thinking. Chew on that for a while!

Taters and Tails

Now you know I don't purposely raise any livestock on my place—I'm strictly flora not fauna (except as by-products of my bountiful gardens).

However, our friends and closest neighbors, Wayve and Dave, live very self-sufficient lives and generously share what they have with others. In the fall we can be assured of a bounty of pig parts from their farm.

We sometimes call this delectable the Commodities Comestibles, or the Stockbrokers Shares. The roasted pigs' tails and home-cut potato chips are washed down with a cold lager. Wayve says, "Just like advice from your broker, this meal is taken with a great deal of salt."

Tongue-Tied Thai

Talk about trendy—even our little town has two Thai restaurants. They are rather small—one is four tables and take-out and the other is take-out only—but nevertheless they have opened some eyes and started some tongues wagging (sorry about that!). I will be the first to say that I have certainly been influenced by my exposure to this fabulous cuisine.

Thin slices of lemon grass and scallions are added at the last minute to the hot steaming broth of the Pork Ball Soup (it is not what you think).

Pork tongues wrapped in bok choy leaves and garnished with enoki mushrooms and red Thai peppers are tied with chive buds and braised to such perfection they will leave you speechless. The golden glow of the curry sauce is subtly enhanced by the tiny yellow flowers of the bok choy.

My youngest brother, Tommy Mac, loves the art and cuisine of Southeast Asia—he's been there. His gold- and blue-bordered plates and etched forks add to the Bangkok ambiance. The Thai silk sash used as a table runner was a gift from a former beau (my husband thinks it would make a good dog leash).

Wormburger

Although the children dreamed up this dynamite sandwich, it is a hearty favorite of adults, too. Sauté a couple of handfuls of red wigglers that you have kept in a bowl of garlic and potatoes for at least twenty-four hours. Add to your regular bean-burger mixture and shape into patties; the wigglers will add a nice crunchy texture to the mushy beans. Dust the patties with cornmeal and fry in a little peanut oil. You will notice the influence of minimalist art in my placement of the primary colors of the cat-sup and mustard. Perfect!

The burger is a snap; it's cutting those potatoes into the waffle shapes the children insist upon that is so difficult and time consuming!

Worms Walking

Just looking at this picture makes me think of those ubiquitous biking shorts made of shiny stretchy fabric that cling unforgivingly to one's hips and upper thighs, sparing not even the smallest indiscretion in one's diet, nor any doubt as to one's gender. For the presentation of my innovative snack for athletes, I have borrowed the charming serving style of the French *pommes frittes* and the English chips. That's the way it goes in the world of food, we are constantly feeding off each other's ideas as well as each other's menus.

"Walking" is diner lingo for "take-out," meaning you pay your money and take your food out of the restaurant to eat it. I'm not sure where you could buy such a delectable treat as this, but the good news is that you can have it for free. Collect the mealworms yourself—even earthworms will do—and feed them the basic potato diet. This item is very high in protein and easy to prepare. Simply sauté the worms very quickly in a little olive oil and salt them lightly before rolling them up in the sports section of the newspaper.

Index